IMAGES
of Sport

WORKINGTON ASSOCIATION FOOTBALL CLUB

Mike Rogan made his Workington debut against Oldham Athletic on 27 December 1966 and stayed with Reds right through to the end of their last Football League season in 1976/77. The Fleetwood-born goalkeeper made 390 Football League appearances for Workington and later played for Stockport County.

IMAGES
of Sport

WORKINGTON ASSOCIATION FOOTBALL CLUB

Paul Eade

TEMPUS

First published 2003

Tempus Publishing Limited
The Mill, Brimscombe Port,
Stroud, Gloucestershire, GL5 2QG

British Library Cataloguing in Publication Data.
A catalogue record for this book is available from the British Library.

ISBN 0 7524 2818 7

Typesetting and origination by Tempus Publishing Limited
Printed in Great Britain by Midway Colour Print, Wiltshire

Contents

About the author

Paul Eade worked for the *Racing Post* in London and Press Association Sport in Leeds before moving to Stockholm in 1999, where he has freelanced for various football websites. In 2002 he wrote *Images of Sport: Scarborough Football Club* in the same Tempus Publishing series as this book.

Acknowledgements

I would like to thank Workington AFC match-day secretary and programme editor Steve Durham for his contributions, assistance and hospitality when I visited the club. Another major contributor was former club groundsman Billy Watson, and I am most grateful to him for allowing me access to his precious archive collection. In addition, Tom Allen and Martin Wingfield kindly allowed me to use materials they had collected for their erstwhile Workington AFC projects. I must also thank The Homes of Football/Stuart Clarke, the Raymond Maule Collection and the *Times & Star* newspaper. In respect of all material, every effort has been made to trace the owner of same and apologies are offered should copyright have inadvertently been infringed.

Introduction

Despite their geographical isolation, the Reds sides of the 1960s gained enormous respect for their attacking football and spent three seasons in the old Third Division. Leaner times followed and the club lost its League status in 1977. However, a devoted band of never-say-die supporters have kept Workington going and, even though attendances these days are often little more than 350, they play at a Borough Park ground little changed from when 21,000 packed in there to watch Manchester United in 1958.

My interest in Workington Association Football Club dates back to the mid-1970s. As a child, despite having no connections with the town, I monitored their results in the hope that Reds could somehow lift themselves above the bottom place in the Fourth Division that they seemed to permanently occupy. Clearly, I had been born to favour the underdog.

It was with despair that, in June 1977, I read that Workington had been voted out of the Football League but, as the years rolled by, I always kept an eye open for their results. During the early 1990s, my interest was re-awakened. Workington were toiling in the lower reaches of the Unibond First Division but, thanks to the *Reds Review* monthly magazines of that period, I became aware that Reds' history was not one of perennial struggle. I read of heady days in the 1960s, when Reds prospered in the Third Division. I learnt of the great League Cup run of 1964/65, when Workington crushed First Division Blackburn Rovers 5-1 at Ewood Park and held Chelsea at home, before gallantly going out in a fifth round replay at Stamford Bridge.

In November 1997, I finally achieved a long-standing ambition of visiting Workington's Borough Park home. If fan loyalty was ever encapsulated absolutely, it was here. A small but devoted band of supporters, despite little reward on the pitch, were battling to keep Workington Reds going in the hope of better times around the corner. The good times finally rolled back into Borough Park for the 1998/99 season. Having, after several previous flirtations, suffered the ignominy of relegation from the Unibond League, Workington bounced back at the first attempt, and won the North West Trains League championship on the last day of the season, following a 14-match unbeaten run. For fans and club officials who had stood by the club through dark days of struggle and attendances barely scraping three figures, it must have been an extraordinarily cathartic experience to witness Reds crowned as champions in front of over 2,200 fans on a fittingly sunny May afternoon.

Given the above facts, it became a natural decision that this book should cover the whole of Workington's history. It would have been easy to cover only the Football League years of 1951 to 1977, but Workington AFC did not die at the Football League AGM on 17 June 1977. The story continues and this, too, is testimony to all those involved with the club. Indeed, as some of these images show, Workington ply their trade at a Borough Park ground that has altered remarkably little since the Football League days. Apart from the very unfortunate semi-dismantlement of the grandstand, Borough Park is pretty much as it was in the 1950s. Without doubt, a trip to Workington is a must for those who have not yet made it. Take in a game under the lights on a Tuesday evening or mid-winter afternoon and to say that you'll feel a hint of nostalgia is an understatement.

The content of this book more or less chose itself. We begin with the pre-Football League days, where available material was very thin on the ground. Next come the early years in the Football League, 1951-1954. The undoubted highlight of Workington's first Football League season was a 1-0 defeat at Liverpool in the FA Cup third round at Anfield in front of 52,581 fans – the biggest crowd the club ever played in front of. Workington finished bottom and second-from-bottom in their first two seasons, but pulled off a something of a coup by securing the services of Bill Shankly as manager on 6 January 1954. Shankly steered Reds clear of what could have been a tricky third re-election vote in 1954 and soon, playing a delightful brand of football, Workington were transformed. Shankly moved on to Huddersfield Town in November 1955, but his contribution was immense, turning Workington into a Football League club to be reckoned with.

Chapter five deals with just one match, arguably the most momentous in Workington's history, when, on 4 January 1958, they hosted Manchester United in the FA Cup third round. A club record crowd of 21,000 crammed into Borough Park as Reds took the lead through Clive Colbridge, before a second-half hat-trick from Dennis Viollet ended Workington's dream. Tragically, the Munich air disaster followed a month later and five of the Manchester United team who played at Workington died.

Chapters six and seven encompass the golden years of Workington in the Football League. After Joe Harvey left to manage Newcastle in the summer of 1962, with Workington having finished eighth in the Fourth Division, it was player-manager Ken Furphy who guided Reds to third place in 1963/64 and promotion to the Third Division. Workington stayed there for just three seasons, but that was an achievement in itself. In chapter eight, we see how Reds came crashing down and had to apply for re-election in 1967 after finishing bottom of the Fourth Division. However, a sixth place attained in 1971/72 indicated that Workington's place still firmly belonged in the Football League.

Chapter nine sadly shows that it was not to be. A succession of re-election applications culminated in a disastrous 1976/77 season, when with only four victories obtained, the writing was on the wall. Chapter ten sees Reds settle fairly comfortably into Non-League life after a shaky start, with respectable finishing positions in the Northern Premier League and some welcome silverware in the President's Cup. However, it was a false dawn and chapter eleven charts some of the grimmest days in Workington's history. The demolition of the grandstand coincided with over a decade of almost unrelenting misery with regular heavy defeats and Reds entrenched in the lower reaches of the Unibond First Division, playing to just a handful of die-hards.

Chapter twelve looks at Workington's rise from the nadir of relegation to the North West Trains League by winning promotion at the first attempt and, finally, chapter thirteen brings us up to the present with Workington back in the Unibond League and in a much healthier state than ten years ago. That Workington will ever again grace the Football League stage has to be considered unlikely. But, given the right circumstances, progress towards playing Conference-level football is not an impossible dream for Workington AFC.

Paul Eade
March 2003

One
The Early Years
1884-1951

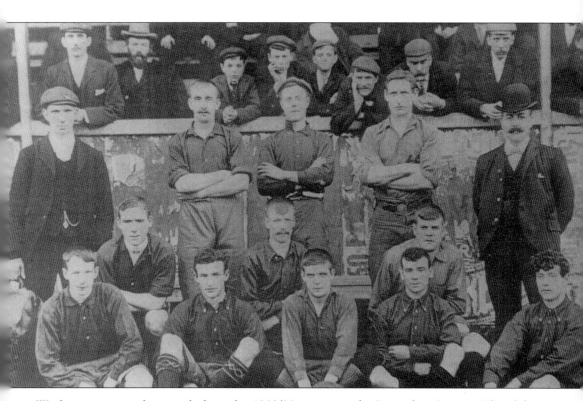

Workington team photograph from the 1902/03 season in the Lancashire League. The club played in six different leagues between 1890 and 1911 before going into liquidation.

Workington Reds A.F.C. 1932-1933.

On reforming in 1921, Workington found more stability, settling into the North Eastern League and playing home games at Lonsdale Park. This line-up is from the 1932/33 season when Reds finished in fifth position in the table.

In 1933/34, a superb FA Cup run saw Workington in the fourth round and hosting Second Division Preston North End.

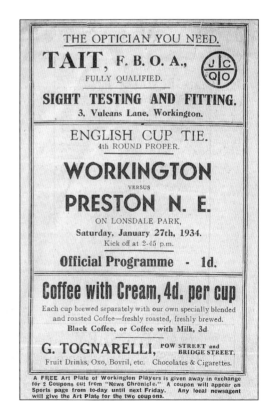

10

Workington take to the field to play Preston North End in the FA Cup on 27 January 1934. Lonsdale Park was clearly filled to capacity as fans can be seen crammed on top of the roof of the building in the background.

As Workington skipper Norman Watson (*right*) prepares for kick-off against Preston North End, dozens of spectators can just be made out perched precariously on the grandstand roof. Preston narrowly won the game 2-1.

Workington rarely finished out of the top five in the North Eastern League in the 1930s. The 1934/35 campaign, from when this picture dates, saw a slightly disappointing eighth placing.

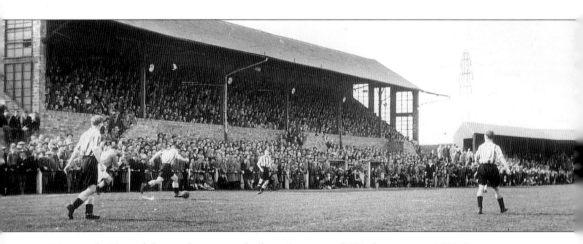

Newcastle United drew a large crowd when they visited Workington in 1949 for a pre-season friendly. As Newcastle launch a counter-attack, Borough Park looks to have attracted a full house.

Joe Harvey (*left*) and Andy Mullen duel for the ball during Newcastle's friendly at Workington in 1949. Harvey was later to manage both clubs with considerable success.

Billy Robson was one of the few players to appear for Workington in both the North Eastern League and the Football League. He played for Reds in the 1950/51 season at the age of just seventeen and stayed at the club until 1960, making 128 Football League appearances and scoring 53 goals.

History of the Club

ASSOCIATION football was first played in Workington in the "60's" and was popularised more fully by the advent of a group of enthusiastic soccer supporters from the Dronfield (Sheffield) area who moved into the Town on the removal to Workington of the Charles Cammell and Co. Steel Works about the year 1884.

From that time onwards Workington played a prominent part in the formation of the Cumberland F.A., were original members of the North-Eastern League and have always striven for the betterment of soccer in the County.

The standard of play in the Cumberland Competitions so improved that Workington sallied forth over the Border and more than held their own against prominent Scottish teams and on their many journeyings to neighbouring Counties returned victorious against teams in the Lancashire and North-Eastern Districts.

As the organisation of the game developed and stable Leagues were formed Workington became members of the Lancashire League and later the Lancashire Combination, which in those days were organisations of high repute. The Club held an honoured position in the Leagues during their membership.

In latter days the Club transferred their affection to the North-Eastern League in which combination the Club has since continued to play. One of the most popular sides on North-Eastern Grounds Workington have gained many honours in the League and Cup Competition of the League.

In the F.A. Cup Competition the Club's record, as previously detailed, is a proud one, and on many occasions Workington has been a team which has progressed in the Competition and has been seen in the Competition Proper, drawn against, and providing strong opposition for, some of the leading sides in the country.

Workington have been holders of the County Senior Cup on many occasions.

Workington is conveniently situate at the junction of the Railway Routes from Carlisle (35 miles), Barrow-in-Furness (66 miles) and Penrith (36 miles) and is adequately served by Rail and Road Services. We are not in an area where we would rob any other League Club of their present supporters.

With a final position of fifth in the North Eastern League in 1951, Workington were ready for Football League membership. A 16-page brochure was produced in support of their application and, as these pages show, it went to great lengths to state their case.

District from which we would draw our Support

The map shows locations across Cumberland including: Allonby, ASPATRIA, Brayton Hall, Allerby, Nealsgate, Crosscanonby, Bullgill, Blennerhassot, Ireby, Burkby, MARYPORT, Dearham, Plumby, Broughton Moor, Dovenby, Armathwaite, Siddick, Papcastle, COCKERMOUTH, Camerton, Brigham, Embleton, Bassenthwaite, Seaton, Great Clifton, Broughton Cross, Stainburn, Bridgefoot, Greysouthen, Eaglesfield, Workington, Lorton, Salterbeck, HARRINGTON, Branthwaite, Dean, Braithwaite, KESWICK, Distington, Ulloch, Portinscale, Oatlands, Wright Green, Lamplugh, Parton, Moresby Parks, Arlecdon, Loweswater, Rowrah, Winder, WHITEHAVEN, Yeathouse, Cleator Moor, Frizington, Moor Row, Cleator, Buttermere, Corkickle, Woodend, St Bees, Egremont, CUMBERLAND.

W EST CUMBERLAND is rich in Mineral Wealth—Coal, Iron Ore, and Limestone. There are over twelve Collieries, nine Iron Ore Mines and six Limestone Quarries. The other part is mostly Agriculture and the Lake District.

In Workington the chief industry is Iron and Steel. The United Steel Co. have large Steel Works and Blast-furnaces employing over 5,000 persons. This firm has its own Dock and Harbour with direct access to their works, so as to cope with vessels of 12,000 tonnage. In addition they have their own Ore Mines, Quarries and Brick and Tar Works in the neighbourhood.

Since 1939 West Cumberland has been completely developed. Thirty-four additional factories are now in operation, and these are nearly all situated in Workington itself or within a seven-mile radius. Labour continues to be absorbed and the present figure of 60,000 employed shows an increase of 33,000 since 1932.

Workington's line-up during the 1950/51 season. From left to right, back row: William Davey (trainer), Albert Leek (director), Ted Cushin, Kenny Wallace, Charles Murray (director), Alan Ford, Bob McAlone, Ted Borthwick, George Creighton, Bobby Williams, Harry Boult (physiotherapist). Front row: Jack Carruthers, Willie Harkness, Jackie Oakes, Billy Robson, Andy Mullen.

Workington's Borough Park ground, the club's home since 1937, was one of the best outside the Football League and, after their good season in the North Eastern League, everything was ready for Reds to take their place in the Football League. At the League AGM on 2 June 1951, Workington AFC were duly elected, with 28 votes, to replace New Brighton, who mustered just 18 votes.

Two
Into the League
1951-1954

Smartly-dressed Workington players at Hagg Hill in Workington at the start of the 1952/53 season. From left to right: Ted Smith (manager), Bob Rooney, Bert Horsley (director), George Dick, Chris Simmonds, Len Hainsworth, -?-, Andy Mullen, Harold Wallbanks, Jock Wallace, Danny McDowell, Alan Ford, Billy Davey (trainer), Jack Vitty, Billy Watson (groundsman).

Official		Programme
1951		1952

Halifax Town.
A.F.C. LTD.

●

Saturday, August 18th
Workington

Kick-off
3-0

Programme for Workington's first game in the Football League, at Halifax on 18 August 1951. Workington lost 3-1 but gave a good account of themselves in front of a 9,326-strong crowd at The Shay.

Workington players line up to meet Mayor Mark Nilsson before the club's first Football League home game against Chesterfield on 22 August 1951. Captain Len Hainsworth is making the introductions.

Workington AFC 1951/52. From left to right, back row: Bert Flatley (manager), Kenny Wallace, Ted Cushin, Bob McAlone, Mick Hardy, Alan Ford, Len Hainsworth, Billy Davey (trainer). Front row: Joe Johnston, Danny McDowall, Chris Simmonds, George Dick, Andy Mullen.

A 3-1 win over Chesterfield, with two goals from Danny McDowell and one from Ted Cushin, gave Reds their first points as a Football League side. The local press put the attendance figure at 15,000.

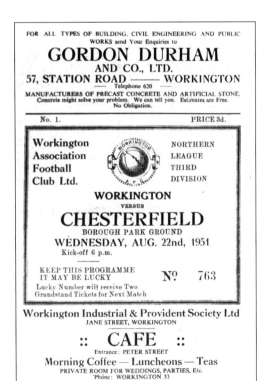

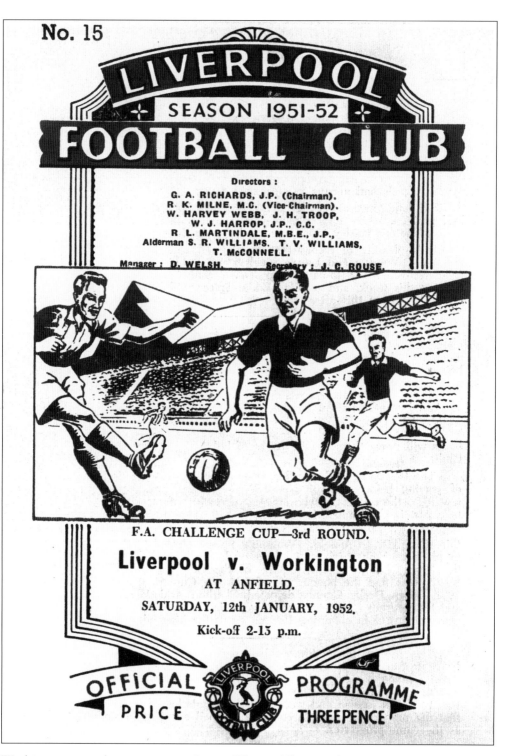

LIVERPOOL

SEASON 1951-52

FOOTBALL CLUB

Directors :
G. A. RICHARDS, J.P. (Chairman).
R. K. MILNE, M.C. (Vice-Chairman).
W. HARVEY WEBB, J. H. TROOP,
W. J. HARROP, J.P. C.C.
R. L. MARTINDALE, M.B.E., J.P.,
Alderman S. R. WILLIAMS, T. V. WILLIAMS,
T. McCONNELL.
Manager : D. WELSH.   Secretary : J. C. ROUSE.

F.A. CHALLENGE CUP—3rd ROUND.

Liverpool v. Workington

AT ANFIELD.

SATURDAY, 12th JANUARY, 1952.

Kick-off 2-15 p.m.

OFFICIAL   PROGRAMME

PRICE   THREEPENCE

Workington scraped a win over non-League Witton Albion in the FA Cup second round, the tie going to a replay. Their reward was a visit to First Division giants Liverpool in the third round on 12 January 1952.

A section of the 3,000 supporters who travelled to Anfield for the FA Cup tie against Liverpool. They made up a small, but passionate section of a gate of 52,581 – by far the biggest attendance that a Workington team have ever played to.

Although Liverpool won the FA Cup third round tie 1-0, Workington went very close to snatching a replay. Liverpool goalkeeper Russell Crossley is at full stretch to keep out this shot from George Dick. These two photographs were scanned from newspaper pages, hence the poor quality, but it was considered worthwhile to include some pictorial record of this historic match.

Sixteen-year-old Jock Wallace in action in goal for Workington against Chesterfield on 13 September 1952. Workington lost 3-2 during a disastrous start to the season that set the tone for the whole campaign.

After finishing second bottom of the Third Division (North) in 1952/53, serious doubts surfaced as to whether the club would gain enough votes to secure re-election. A vigorous campaign was launched with this leaflet being distributed to the chairmen and directors of other clubs. In the end, Workington secured 36 votes over the 16 for applicants Wigan Athletic, but it gave clear indication that Reds could not afford to risk a bottom four placing the following season.

FROM

WORKINGTON A.F.C.
LTD.

TO THE

CHAIRMAN
AND
DIRECTORS
OF

.... A. F. C.

PLEASE STUDY CAREFULLY

George Aitken. Signed from Middlesbrough in the summer of 1953, Aitken was destined to become one of Workington's all-time greats. The centre half played 262 Football League games for Reds before becoming club trainer in the summer of 1960. After six and a half years as assistant manager at Watford, Aitken returned to Workington as manager from 1971 to 1975.

Workington AFC, 1953/54. From left to right, back row: Ted Cushin, George Aitken, Dennis Stokoe, Malcolm Newlands, Rex Dunlop, Jack Vitty. Front row: Norman Mitchell, Joe Johnson, Jimmy Dailey, Chris Simmonds, Hugh Cameron.

When Workington got off to a bad start in the 1953/54 season, the board of directors realised they had to act to preserve the club's Football League status. A clutch of new signings included Rex Dunlop, a left-sided player from Glasgow Rangers. Dunlop went on to make 110 appearances for Workington, scoring some important goals.

Norman Mitchell was another Reds signing after he had come to the club's notice by scoring a hat-trick for West Stanley against Workington Reserves. Pictured here on his debut for Workington Reserves at Lonsdale Park – note the greyhound track running rails in the background – the winger notched up 150 appearances for Workington before joining Hartlepool in March 1958.

Goalkeeper Malcolm Newlands repels a Ferryhill Athletic raid during the FA Cup first round tie at Borough Park on 21 November 1953. Workington won 3-0, but went on to lose 2-1 at Stockport County in the second round.

Sir Stanley Matthews visited Borough Park in 1953 in connection with a newspaper article that he was writing. From left to right: E.D. Smith (chairman), comedian Charlie Chester, Tommy Jones (trainer), Sir Stanley Matthews, Bert Horsley, Reg Scaife.

Jimmy Dailey. Dailey's signing in December 1953 was something of a coup, and one of the best made by the club during the decade. Having been a prolific marksman for Sheffield Wednesday and Birmingham City, Dailey did not disappoint, scoring on his Workington debut against York City on 19 December 1953. He went on to score 84 League goals in 176 appearances and, in 1985, was voted Reds' all-time favourite player by readers of the *West Cumberland Times & Star*.

Three
Shankly at Workington
1954-1955

Jack Vitty (*right*) battles for the ball during the 5-1 defeat of Hartlepool on 24 August 1955. During his short tenure as manager at Workington, Bill Shankly transformed Reds from perennial strugglers to a competent Football League outfit.

Bill Shankly resigned as manager at Grimsby on 2 January 1954 and became Workington boss on 6 January 1954. It was a momentous appointment that almost certainly saved Workington's status as a Football League club, as Shankly immediately turned the ailing side's fortunes around.

Workington v. Chester on 16 January 1954. This Norman Mitchell header put Reds on their way to a 2-0 victory – their first win under Shankly.

Bill Shankly leads a training session at Borough Park in 1954. Shankly revolutionised the coaching methods at the club and quickly steered the side out of the re-election zone in the Third Division (North).

Workington's progress under Bill Shankly was highlighted when they beat League leaders Port Vale at Borough Park in front of a 14,000-strong crowd on 6 February 1954. The line-up for that game was, from left to right, back row: Ted Cushin, Dennis Stokoe, Jack Vitty, Malcolm Newlands, Rex Dunlop, George Aitken. Front row: Norman Mitchell, Joe Johnson, Jimmy Dailey, Ian Winters, Hugh Cameron.

Bill Shankly's first signing as Workington manager was forward Ernie Whittle (*front row, standing*) from Lincoln in March 1954. Whittle made an immediate impact, scoring 6 goals before the end of the season, and he went on to find the net 44 times in 110 appearances for the Reds.

Norman Mitchell scores Workington's first goal in the 2-0 victory over Grimsby Town on 17 March 1954. The win edged Reds away from the re-election zone and, despite a spate of injuries, the side accomplished their mission by finishing in twentieth place.

Stewart McCallum, Rex Dunlop and Ken Rose at Borough Park in 1954. McCallum and Rose only played 16 matches between them during short stays at the club, with the former moving to Rhyl early in 1956.

Jack Vitty (*left*) prepares to captain Workington in their FA Cup first round tie against Cheshire County League side Hyde United on 20 November 1954. Reds ran out easy 5-1 winners in front of a 10,193-strong crowd.

WORKINGTON A.F.C. LTD.

Club Colours : Red Shirts, White Knickers
Members of Football Association, Cumberland F. A., Football League, Division III (North),
N.E. Football League

Chairman : E. D. SMITH	Registered Office and Ground
Manager : W. SHANKLY	BOROUGH PARK
Financial Secretary : J. QUAYLE	WORKINGTON
General Secretary : H. HORSLEY	Telephone Workington 871

Monday January 17th 1955.

Reg Drury Esq.,
Sport,
9,Stamford Street,
London.S.E.I.

Dear Reg,

Thanks for paper,actually,I lost my copy on the way home last Sunday.

Note your remarks on Page 5,and I'm in complete agreement with you,this being good losers,is being exagerated.We were good losers at Luton,but although outwardly I took the defeat well,inwardly I was boiling,I have no time for losing Reg,and I'm possessed with a killer instinct,which in my playing days paid dividends, without using shady tactics,I made sure that my immediate opponent drew a blank.I used to think, that it would be better to die,than lose,to enable me to reach the top,and keep their,I went to all extremes,no woman,no smoking,early to bed, good food,this went on for years,but it was worth while.If all players in the game did the same,the game would improve,and would reach such a high standard,that it would really be a honour to be defeated.

You will be thinking I'm blowing a trumpet,instead of giving my opinion,of your article,but its perfectly honest.Hope you are well Reg.All good wishes. Yours sincerely,

Bill

Letter from Bill Shankly to *The People*'s sports editor Reg Drury on 17 January 1955. The content provides a fascinating insight into Shankly's philosophy, notably the phrase 'I used to think it would be better to die, than lose.' Ten months later, Bill Shankly left Workington to become assistant manager at Huddersfield.

Four

Football League Stability
1955-1958

Bill Robson and Clive Colbridge both fail to connect with a Tommy Kinloch pass in the League match against Bradford City on 25 September 1957.

Malcolm Newlands is beaten in the Workington goal as Jack Vitty and Jimmy Fleming look on helplessly in the Third Division (North) game at Darlington on 17 March 1956. Goals from Jack Bertolini and Billy Robson gave Reds a point in a 2-2 draw at Feethams.

Workington AFC 1956/57. The club finished an excellent fourth in the Third Division (North) From left to right, back row: Joe Wilson, Jack Vitty, Malcolm Newlands, Tommy Kinloch, George Aitken, Tucker Finlay. Front row: Ernie Whittle, Jackie Bertolini, Jimmy Dailey, Ken Chisholm, Des Jones.

Former Dundee United, Falkirk and Carlisle United half-back Tommy Kinloch signed for Workington in the summer of 1956. His experience proved vital in the 1956/57 campaign but, after 70 appearances and 12 goals, the Scot moved on to Southport in February 1958.

Ken Chisholm. Signed by manager Norman Low from Sunderland on the eve of the 1956/57 season, Chisholm chipped in with 12 goals during the following campaign, despite injury problems. He was, however, involved in a long-running saga over allegedly improper transfer payments and, in February 1958, he left to become manager of Glentoran.

Tommy Kinloch, Jack Vitty, Jackie Bertolini, George Aitken and Bobby Brown exercise at Borough Park in the 1956/57 season. Brown came to Workington from Motherwell during the summer of 1956 and stayed until 1968, making a record 419 Football League appearances.

Jack Vitty (*in white*) clears in front of goalkeeper Malcolm Newlands in a Third Division (North) game at Bradford City, sometime in the mid-1950s.

Alex Rollo. Pictured here outside Borough Park sometime in the 1970s, Rollo was Joe Harvey's only signing before the 1957/58 fixtures got underway. Rollo had played over 50 games for Glasgow Celtic, and he was a fixture for Workington at left-back until May 1960, when he joined Sligo Rovers.

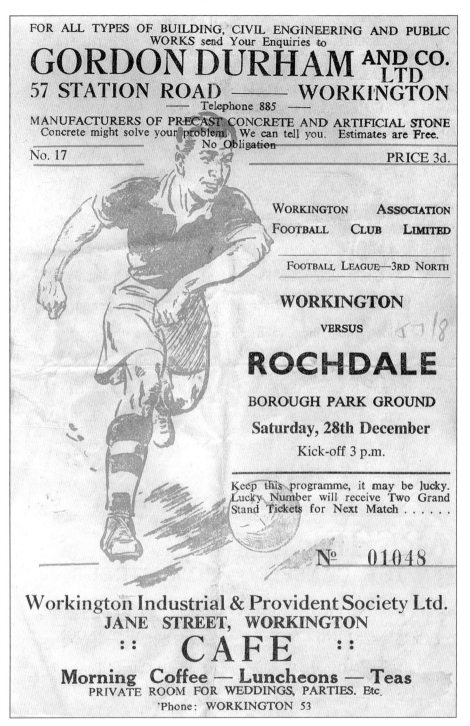

No. 17   PRICE 3d.

WORKINGTON   ASSOCIATION
FOOTBALL   CLUB   LIMITED

FOOTBALL LEAGUE—3RD NORTH

WORKINGTON

VERSUS

ROCHDALE

BOROUGH PARK GROUND

Saturday, 28th December

Kick-off 3 p.m.

Keep this programme, it may be lucky.
Lucky Number will receive Two Grand
Stand Tickets for Next Match . . . . . .

Nᵒ   01048

Programme for the Third Division (North) game between Workington and Rochdale on
28 December 1957. This was the last home match before the club were to face Manchester
United in the FA Cup third round and it informed fans 'all tickets sold, no money taken' for
what was to be one of the biggest games in Workington's history.

Joe Harvey (*left*) is pictured with long-serving Workington groundsman Billy Watson. After Norman Low quit as Workington boss in February 1957, Harvey was persuaded to leave Barrow to become the new Reds manager before the start of the 1957/58 campaign.

Ted Purdon (*on the ground*) narrowly misses a chance for Workington at Borough Park some time in 1957, with Tommy Kinloch looking on in anguish. Manager Norman Low went to great lengths to sign Purdon from Sunderland, but the forward played just 33 games for Reds before being sold to Barrow for £6,000 in March 1958 after a fall-out with Low's successor Joe Harvey.

Five

Reds versus
the Busby Babes
January 1958

Clive Colbridge (*right*) and Duncan Edwards chase a loose ball during Workington's FA Cup third round tie against Manchester United on 4 January 1958 in front of a record crowd of 21,000.

Cup fever hit Workington as soon as they drew Manchester United in the FA Cup third round. The game was sold out long before the 3 p.m. kick-off on 4 January 1958.

Clive Colbridge shot Workington into a shock sixth-minute lead, and Manchester United looked shaky in the first twenty minutes at Borough Park. United 'keeper Harry Gregg struggles to deal with a Workington raid, with Workington's Billy Robson (8) lurking and Roger Byrne on the goal-line.

Workington forward Ted Purdon on the attack, with United's Roger Byrne closing in. Billy Robson runs on in anticipation.

A section of the crowd on Workington's biggest day at Borough Park. The official attendance was given as 21,000, although later estimates put the figure at 19,000, when it emerged that many tickets allocated to Manchester United had not been used.

Ken Chisholm runs in for Reds, but United 'keeper Harry Gregg has the ball covered. United's Duncan Edwards (*left*) and Mark Jones look on.

Clive Colbridge and United's Bill Foulkes tussle for the ball in front of a packed Popular Side at Borough Park.

Workington goalkeeper Malcolm Newlands pulls off a fine save, with Bobby Charlton in the left of the picture. Workington held on to their 1-0 lead until half-time, and an upset looked on the cards.

A quick-fire second-half hat-trick from Dennis Viollet (10) extinguished Workington's FA Cup dream, but the home side battled to the end and the game finished at 3-1 to Manchester United. Late in the game, United goalkeeper Harry Gregg receives attention for an injury, with Duncan Edwards and Roger Byrne (3) looking on. Bobby Charlton is partly hidden in the background. The Workington players are Ted Purdon (*left*) and Jack Bertolini.

Workington's payment to Manchester United of one-third of the gate receipts plus travelling expenses. Tragically, one month after the match, the Munich air disaster killed half of the Manchester United 'Busby Babes' team, including five who had played at Borough Park – Roger Byrne, Duncan Edwards, Eddie Colman, Mark Jones and Tommy Taylor.

Six

Prosperity and Promotion 1958-1964

The Workington side that beat Barrow 3-1 at Borough Park on 3 September 1960. From left to right, back row: Bobby Brown, Jackie Hinchliffe, Keith Burkinshaw, Charlie Wright, Roy Tennant, Barry Gibb. Front row: Noel Hodgson, Peter Harburn, Tommy Brownlee, Tommy Dixon, Frank Kirkup.

Roy Tennant joined Workington from Brighton in the summer of 1958, with Jack Bertolini moving in the opposite direction. The swap proved fruitful, as Tennant went to play over 150 games in Workington's defence before emigrating to South Africa in January 1962.

Workington used four different goalkeepers in the first half of the 1958/59 season. Billy Frame, signed from Dumfries, took over the number 1 jersey at the end of January 1959 and played 9 successive matches, but when Malcolm Newlands returned in March, it was to signal the end of his brief Borough Park career.

After finishing seventeenth in the newly-formed Fourth Division in 1958/59, manager Joe Harvey decided to rebuild the team for the 1959/60 season. This programme for the opening game of the season against Southport shows two of the eight new faces – Frank Kirkup, signed from Blackburn Rovers, and Colin Keir, a winger transferred from Portsmouth.

Bob Morrison, signed from Nottingham Forest, was an instant success at Borough Park, finishing as top goalscorer in the 1959/60 season. However, despite his 17 goals, the new-look Workington side could only finish in sixteenth place in the Fourth Division.

Charlie Wright joined Workington from Glasgow Rangers in July 1958 at the age of nineteen. He became first-choice goalkeeper at the start of the 1960/61 season and made 123 League appearances for Reds, before joining Grimsby Town for £10,000 in February 1963.

Harry Anders (*left*) with Bobby Morrison and Bobby Brown in the dugout at Borough Park during the 1960/61 season. Anders was a vastly experienced winger who had played for Preston North End, Manchester City and Accrington Stanley. However, he played just 7 matches for Workington and left in the summer of 1961 to join Runcorn.

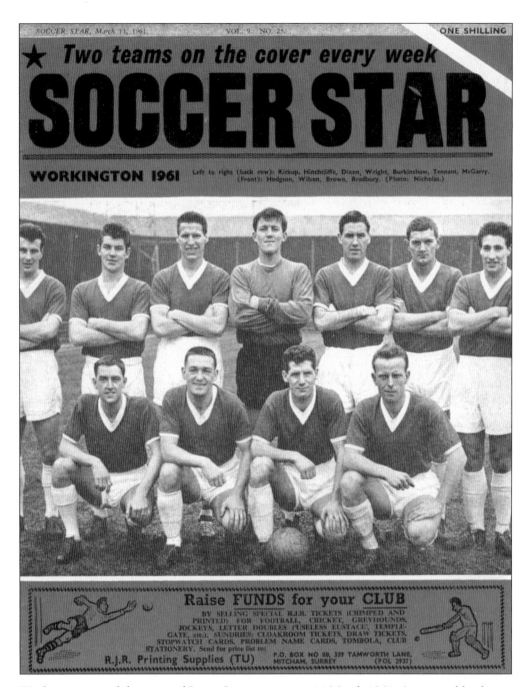

SOCCER STAR, March 11, 1961. VOL. 9. NO. 25. ONE SHILLING

★ **Two teams on the cover every week**

SOCCER STAR

WORKINGTON 1961 Left to right (back row): Kirkup, Hinchcliffe, Dixon, Wright, Burkinshaw, Tennant, McGarry. (Front): Hodgson, Wilson, Brown, Bradbury. (Photo: Nicholas.)

Raise FUNDS for your CLUB

BY SELLING SPECIAL R.J.R. TICKETS (CRIMPED AND PRINTED) FOR FOOTBALL, CRICKET, GREYHOUNDS, JOCKEYS, LETTER DOUBLES ('USELESS EUSTACE', TEMPLE-GATE, etc.). SUNDRIES: CLOAKROOM TICKETS, DRAW TICKETS, STOPWATCH CARDS, PROBLEM NAME CARDS, TOMBOLA, CLUB STATIONERY. Send for price list to:

R.J.R. Printing Supplies (TU) P.O. BOX NO 80, 339 TAMWORTH LANE, MITCHAM, SURREY (POL 2937)

Workington graced the cover of *Soccer Star* magazine on 11 March 1961. A respectable placing of eighth was attained during the 1960/61 season, but the club were hampered by very disappointing attendances, with only 1,750 turning up for the visit of Southport on 25 March.

Manager Joe Harvey leads by example during a snowy training session at Borough Park ahead of Nottingham Forest's visit for the FA Cup third round on 6 January 1962. Forest won a keenly contested match 2-1, with Ron McGarry on target for Workington.

Barry Lowes. Lowes was the first signing by new player-manager Ken Furphy, who agreed to take over the helm at Borough Park in July 1962.

John Lumsden was another new face at Borough Park early in 1962, signing from Aston Villa where he had been a regular in the reserves for four seasons. Lumsden became a fixture at centre half for Workington, at one stage playing in 142 consecutive games – he went on to play in 287 in total. He finally left for Chesterfield in March 1968.

Scot Jimmy Moran was signed from Darlington for £2,000 during the summer of 1963. The left-sided midfielder proved to be a key addition to the team, and he was ever-present in Reds' 1963/64 campaign.

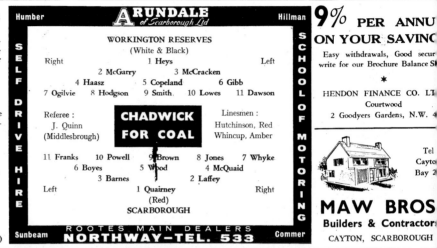

Humber   Hillman

WORKINGTON RESERVES
(White & Black)

Right   1 Heys   Left

2 McGarry   3 McCracken

4 Haasz   5 Copeland   6 Gibb

7 Ogilvie   8 Hodgson   9 Smith   10 Lowes   11 Dawson

Referee :   Linesmen :
J. Quinn   Hutchinson, Red
(Middlesbrough)   Whincup, Amber

CHADWICK FOR COAL

11 Franks   10 Powell   9 Brown   8 Jones   7 Whyke
6 Boyes   5 Wood   4 McQuaid
3 Barnes   2 Laffey

Left   1 Quairney   Right
(Red)
SCARBOROUGH

S E L F   D R I V E   H I R E

S C H O O L   O F   M O T O R I N G

ARUNDALE of Scarborough Ltd

Sunbeam   ROOTES MAIN DEALERS   Commer
NORTHWAY—TEL. 533

Workington reserves helped re-form the previously long-established North Eastern League in 1962, which had earlier folded when the Football League reserve teams broke away to form their own competition. A rather complicated format saw the North Eastern League and the North Eastern League Cup both played as mini-leagues. This Workington reserves side that travelled to Scarborough on 27 October 1962 lost 4-2, despite including several first-teamers.

Brian Clough visited Borough Park in November 1963 for a testimonial game for Workington's Keith Burkinshaw. Burkinshaw had played for the club since joining from Liverpool in December 1957, and he made over 300 appearances for the Reds.

A 1-1 draw at Barrow on 18 January 1964 kept Workington in the promotion-chasing pack.
Mike Commons wins a header, with Dave Carr looking on.

Barry Lowes was instrumental in Workington's promotion push in 1963/64. A speedy
winger, signed from Blackpool for £3,500
in August 1962, his game matured at
Borough Park.

THE MANAGER WRITES

Well, apart from freak results this week-end, we have finally made it into Division Three. The team have put in a fantastic run since our home defeat by Halifax and in gaining promotion they have confounded the many critics who for years have said that the club did not want promotion.

After 12 years in the lower Divisions it is indeed a happy and proud moment for me, not especially as the Manager, but that I have been associated with and played in a team that has been a team in every sense of the word. At this time it is usual for the Manager and team to be given most of the praise, but I would like to express my thanks to George Aitken, our trainer, for his loyal support in everything I have tried to do, to John Curwen, assistant trainer, for the hard work he has put in, not only with the Reserve team, but for his co-operation with George Barnes, our Junior official, in the running of the Junior sides, to Keith Burkinshaw, player coach, for his assistance throughout the season as well as his performances on the field and to all the administrative, ground and catering staff.

A big thank you also to the supporters who have had faith in the "Reds" and given us their loyal support through all the ups and downs.

To new friends, we I hope you will come again next year and help us with your support to stay in the Third Division.

I am already looking forward to the visits from our Carlisle neighbours who of course have made a swift and triumphant return to the Third Division and to whom I offer the congratulations of the Workington Directors, officials and players. **KEN FURPHY**

A goal-less draw with Exeter at Borough Park on 25 April 1964 secured third place in the Fourth Division. It was an extraordinary achievement by Furphy, who had built a winning side despite having very little money to spend on players.

58

Seven

At the Height of their Powers 1964-1966

Geoff Martin is ready to pounce, but Port Vale goalkeeper Ken Hancock hangs on to the ball in Workington's Third Division debut at Borough Park on 22 August 1964.

A young Mike Rogan (*left*) and Keith Burkinshaw paint the girders on the Popular Side enclosure, probably in the summer of 1964. Rogan was to make his debut in goal for Reds in December 1966.

Workington made an explosive Third Division debut by thrashing Port Vale 4-1 at Borough Park. Kit Napier (*foreground*) scored on his debut, as did Geoff Martin (*background*). Barry Lowes and Dave Carr were also on the mark.

REFEREE:
H. G. WILSON
STOCKTON

WORKINGTON

Ian Ower

Ken Furphy (2)   John Lumsden (3)

Dixie Hale (4)   Robert Brown (5)   Keith Burkinshaw (6)

Dave Carr (8)   Jimmy Moran (10)

Barry Lowes (7)   Kit Napier (9)   Geoff Martin (11)

BALL DONATED BY
Mr. TOM DONOCKLEY, BOOKMAKER, 10, CURWEN ST.

11	10	9	8	7
Harrison	Douglas	Byrom	McEvoy	Ferguson
	6		5	4
	McGrath	England		Clayton
		3	2	
		Joyce	Newton	
		Else		

LINESMEN:
A. CALLENDER
D. PRITCHARD

BLACKBURN R.

After beating Barrow by a competition record 9-1 in the League Cup first round, followed by winning 1-0 at Scunthorpe in the second round, Workington pulled out a plum by drawing First Division Blackburn Rovers at home in the third round. Blackburn's side was littered with internationals, including former England captain Ronnie Clayton and Republic of Ireland regular Mick McGrath.

Workington's Kit Napier and Blackburn Rovers' Keith Newton in an aerial duel during the League Cup third round game at Borough Park on 14 October 1964.

Reds weathered an early storm to take the game to their First Division opponents in the second half, with Geoff Martin hitting the post, but the match ended goal-less. Martin and Dave Carr (8) put the Blackburn defence under pressure, with Ronnie Clayton an anxious spectator.

A very rare single-sheet official programme
issued for the League Cup third round replay
between Blackburn Rovers and Workington
on 22 October 1964.

ROVERS GO OUT IN DISGRACE

THE ROVERS made a sorry mess of last night's League Cup third round replay against Third Division Workington at Ewood and suffered yet another ignominious exit from this competition.

They had the incentive of a home tie against Norwich City in the next stage but staggered to a 5—1 defeat, after being three down at half-time. It was a disgraceful, dispirited exhibition which undid all the good of last Saturday.

Scarcely a man did himself any credit, and their weakest links were their internationals. They were outpaced and outmanoeuvred by superior opposition and got the slow handicap from their own fans.

On a pitch affected by torrential pre-match rain the lethargic, over-casual Rovers had a rude early shock when Workington's brisk challenge brought them a goal after 10 minutes. Their left back Lumsden beat England in the air with a forward lob and centre forward Napier dashed through to shoot in off the post as Else met him.

A grand run by the debutant Horrey, a fast direct raider,

promised a Rovers reply, but his backward centre came to nothing. A long dribble by Douglas ended tamely; in his next attack he drove yards wide.

It was undoubtedly Workington's first half and the Blackburn defence got into a hopeless tangle after 36 minutes for Napier to score again from a right wing cross.

Only Else's daring prevented Napier completing a first half hat-trick; instead, inside right Carr got the third after 43 minutes, from close in.

No doubt the Rovers got an interval dressing down from manager Marshall. At least it brought out more spirit and after an hour's play a long cross by Newton was partially cleared and McEvoy hit the rebound on the turn to score by way of the crossbar.

The Rovers now shot hard and often; but usually wide.

It was Workington who got the next two goals both by right winger Lowes.

Attendance: 6,282.

W. W.

Workington defied all expectations
by not only winning at Ewood Park
but by doing with a score-line of
5-1, thereby recording one of the
greatest results in their history. The
Blackburn Times records how Rovers
were 'outpaced and outmanoeuvred
by superior opposition'.

Keith Burkinshaw took over as player-manager at Workington immediately after the departure of Ken Furphy to manage Watford in November 1964.

Ken Furphy's departure came in the midst of a 13-game unbeaten run for Workington that lifted them into third place in the Third Division. Oldham 'keeper Ronnie Swan punches clear to keep Geoff Martin (*partly hidden*) at bay during the 0-0 draw at Borough Park on 21 November 1964.

Burkinshaw's Reds. From left to right, back row: Geoff Martin, John Lumsden, Ian Ower, Bobby Brown, John Ogilvie, Kit Napier. Front row: Barry Lowes, Dixie Hale, Keith Burkinshaw (player-manager), Dave Carr, Jimmy Moran.

Workington were in unstoppable form, and a 3-0 win over Second Division Norwich City was rewarded by the visit of London giants Chelsea in the League Cup fifth round. Chelsea raced into a 2-0 lead, but Reds produced a stirring comeback, with goals from Dave Carr and Kit Napier earning a replay at Stamford Bridge.

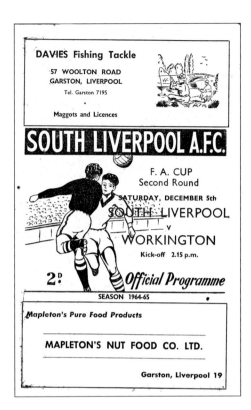

SOUTH LIVERPOOL A.F.C.

F. A. CUP
Second Round

SATURDAY, DECEMBER 5th

SOUTH LIVERPOOL
v
WORKINGTON

Kick-off 2.15 p.m.

2ᴰ   *Official Programme*

SEASON 1964-65

Workington paid a rare visit to Holly Park to play South Liverpool in the FA Cup second round on 5 December 1964. On a waterlogged pitch, Jimmy Moran settled the game for Workington with two second-half goals.

On a gloomy night at Stamford Bridge, Workington held Chelsea for 80 minutes before two Peter Osgood goals sealed the tie for the home side. Reds' superb cup triumphs against Blackburn Rovers and Norwich and their achievement in taking Chelsea to a replay, coupled with scintillating League form that took them up to third place in the Third Division, were arguably the best two months in Workington AFC's history.

Stamford Bridge Grounds
LONDON SW6

LEAGUE CHAMPIONS 1954-55

CHELSEA
FOOTBALL CLUB

FOOTBALL LEAGUE CUP
FIFTH ROUND (REPLAY)
SEASON 1964-65

Wednesday, 16th December, 1964

CHELSEA
v
WORKINGTON

KICK-OFF 7.30 p.m.

OFFICIAL PROGRAMME — SIXPENCE

THE FOOTBALL LEAGUE CUP
®
Winners
1960-61 Aston Villa
1961-62 Norwich City
1962-63 Birmingham City
1963-64 Leicester City

Workington AFC, 1965. The second half of the 1964/65 season turned into an anti-climax. Reds' form fell away and, in March 1965, Keith Burkinshaw resigned after chairman E.D. Smith interfered in team selection. Workington settled for a final position of fifteenth in the Third Division. From left to right, back row: John Lumsden, John Chapman, Ian Ower, Dixie Hale, John Ogilvie, Clive Middlemass. Front row: Barry Lowes, Ken Oliver, Kit Napier, Jimmy Moran, Geoff Martin.

Ken Oliver in flight against Swindon on 11 September 1965. Reds made an uncertain start to the 1965/66 campaign under new manager George Ainsley, and they lost this encounter at Borough Park 3-0.

Dixie Hale lets fly in Workington's 6-1 thrashing of Exeter City on 9 October 1965. From mid-September until early October, Reds played some fearless attacking football, winning 6-1 at Swansea and again crushing Swansea 7-0, just five days before the Exeter match.

Kit Napier, signed from Preston North End in 1964, scored hat-tricks against Exeter and Swansea (twice), including a four-goal haul in the home Swansea fixture, and it was no surprise when Newcastle paid £20,000 for his signature in November 1965.

Workington embarked on another League Cup run in 1965/66, beating Brentford and Stockport County, before drawing Second Division Ipswich Town at home in the third round. Here Peter Foley wins a header during the game at Borough Park on 13 October 1965. The match ended 1-1, and Workington went on to succumb 3-1 in the replay at Portman Road.

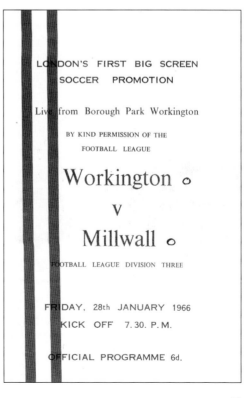

LONDON'S FIRST BIG SCREEN
SOCCER PROMOTION

Live from Borough Park Workington

BY KIND PERMISSION OF THE
FOOTBALL LEAGUE

Workington o

v

Millwall o

FOOTBALL LEAGUE DIVISION THREE

FRIDAY, 28th JANUARY 1966

KICK OFF 7.30. P.M.

OFFICIAL PROGRAMME 6d.

Workington participated in one of the first closed-circuit televised matches when they hosted Millwall on 28 January 1966. Four giant screens were erected at the Den, and over 9,000 fans watched the game in London. This is the Millwall issue of the programme for the game that ended 0-0.

Barry Lowes was instrumental in Workington's fine form in the first half of the 1965/66 season. However, several clubs became interested in the forward and an offer of £10,000 plus Billy Griffin in February 1966 was impossible for the Workington board to refuse.

George Ainsley was quick to bring in new faces after Barry Lowes' departure, and one of his most interesting early signings was Australian forward Max Tolson, who went on to play regularly for his country and was in the Australia 1974 World Cup finals squad in Germany. From left to right, back row: John Lumsden, Peter Foley, Geoff Martin, Ian Ower, Clive Middlemass, Billy Griffin, Ken Oliver. Front row: Dave Butler, Dixie Hale, Bobby Brown, Max Tolson, John Ogilvie. Workington's final position of fifth in the Third Division in 1965/66 is their highest final placing in the Football League.

Eight
Signs of Struggle
1966-1973

Billy Griffin (*partly hidden*) and Eddie Holliday play in a match at Borough Park in 1967. With Reds finishing bottom of the Third Division in 1966/67 and then second bottom of the Fourth Division in 1967/68, a long period of almost uninterrupted struggle commenced.

John Ogilvie. Signed from Blackpool as a nineteen-year-old in July 1962, Ogilvie converted from a winger to a full-back and never looked back. He became a regular fixture in Workington's line-ups right through to his retirement at the end of the 1974/75 season, amassing over 400 appearances for the Reds.

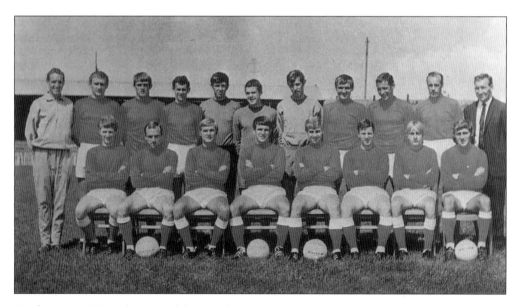

Workington AFC at the start of the 1968/69 season. From left to right, back row: John Lattimer (physiotherapist), John Ogilvie, Tom Spencer, Clive Middlemass, Mike Rogan, John Burridge, Mike Williams, Eddie Holliday, Tony Geidmintis, Gerry Graham, Brian Doyle (manager). Front row: Eric Banks, Alan Tyrer, Bobby Greig, Dave Butler, Brian Tinnion, Derek Trail, Barry Jewell, John McGettigan.

CLUB CALL

WORKINGTON F.C.
Borough Park,
Workington,
Cumberland.

PUT a line across England from Preston to Hull and only 18 of The League's 92 clubs are in the large area from there to the Tweed. Workington are one of the four nearest the border. This geographical remoteness, plus the problems of trying to run an Association team successfully in a hotbed of Rugby League interest, is the main reason why Workington are a struggling club in a sparsely populated area.

☐ All things considered, the enthusiasm of the soccer addicts there is a matter for wonderment. In 17 League seasons Workington, much more often than not, have stayed in the lower half of the table. Their highest position in the Northern Section of the former Division Three was fourth in 1956–57, with 58 points.

☐ One point more four years ago put Workington in the new Third Division along with their Carlisle neighbours. Alas, their stay was short. They plummeted from fifth position (52 points) in their second season to bottom place (31 points). Only once—in their initial League season—have they finished with a lower total.

☐ Worse followed. Last season Workington, again with 31 points, finally occupied the position next to the bottom and were re-elected for the third time. They are among those impecunious clubs who increasingly are having to depend on faith, hope and chance (as represented by pools, lucky numbers, "golden goals" and kindred money-raising efforts).

☐ Their gates today are not a fraction of the League record of 19,200 established in the "local derby" with Carlisle in 1952 (a year after they gained a League place at the expense of New Brighton in the old Third Division north. In recent years, too, managers have come and gone. This season Brian Doyle has taken over from Frank Upton and there are countless well-wishers crossing their fingers for this plucky club in a soccer outpost.

The Club Badge.

Director-Secretary
Herbert Horsley.

Team manager
Brian Doyle

ADVERSITY MOST OF THE WAY

SUCH MODEST fame as Workington have achieved since the club's reorganisation in 1921 took it beyond the limited range of Cumberland competitions is chronicled in F.A. Cup rather than Football League records.

☐ Success in the qualifying stages took the "Reds" of this northern coal-mining town into the first round proper in successive seasons during the 1920's and inspired an application for League status.

☐ To Workington's chagrin, the 1929 annual meeting did not give them a single vote, but in the F.A. Cup the team still periodically attracted attention. In 1934 Preston North End had to fight desperately before narrowly winning a fourth round tie at Workington. Two seasons later a then strong Bradford (P.A.) team won a home tie by only the odd goal. Workington by 1948 had battled into the competition proper five more times, and once reached the second round by winning at Lincoln.

☐ The peak was reached in 1952 when mighty Liverpool were held to a 1–0 win at Anfield. Twice again in the 1950's Workington advanced to the third round, with Manchester United's visit in 1958 the greatest attraction in the club's history. A record crowd for the ground, 21,000, saw the great team which was largely wiped out by the Munich tragedy a few weeks later win by 3–1.

Brian Doyle took over from Frank Upton as manager at the start of the 1968/69 season. This excerpt from the *Football League Review* shows the uphill task he faced in terms of crowds, geography and finance, in bringing success to Borough Park.

Workington occasionally trained at the local Stainburn Secondary School if bad weather prevented them from using the facilities at Borough Park.

Workington at Gillford Park, Carlisle. From left to right, back row: Tony Geidmintis, Dave Butler, Clive Middlemass, Mike Rogan, John Burridge, Brian Doyle (manager), Mike Williams, John Ogilvie, Joe Wilson, Tom Spencer, John Lattimer. Front row: Derek Trail, Alan Tyrer, Peter Barlow, Tommy Spratt, Eric Banks, Johnny Martin.

Clive Middlemass. A key midfielder for Workington throughout the latter part of the 1960s, Middlemass' career was cruelly cut short after a car crash, and he was forced to retire in 1970 at the age of just twenty-five. Middlemass later went into management, including a lengthy spell in charge at Carlisle United.

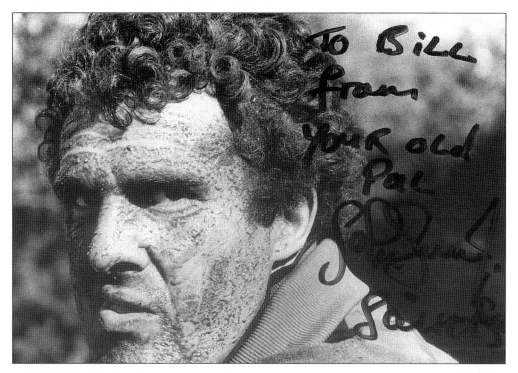

John Burridge became one of the best-known footballers to come from Workington. Beginning his career as a teenager at his hometown club, the goalkeeper made 27 League appearances for Reds before moving to Blackpool for £10,000 in April 1971. His subsequent lengthy career saw Burridge make over 800 appearances in senior football, including with, amongst many others, Sheffield United, Wolves and Manchester City.

Alan Tyrer. In Everton's first team at the age of seventeen, Tyrer also had a spell at Arsenal and joined Workington in 1968, after having played for Mansfield and Bury. He had two spells at Borough Park and made 228 League appearances for the Reds up to 1975/76.

Mike Rogan made the number 1 jersey his own for most of Workington's latter years in the Football League. He graduated through the youth ranks and stayed with Reds through until June 1977, making over 400 first-team appearances.

Workington's players take a stroll outside the Grand Hotel in Scarborough prior to the FA Cup first round tie against the Northern Premier League side on 21 November 1970. From left to right: Tommy Spratt, Alan Tyrer, Les Massie, Dave Helliwell, Brian Doyle (manager), John Lattimer, John Burridge, Dave Irving, Johnny Martin, Jimmy Goodfellow, Joe Wilson. John Burridge played briefly for Scarborough some twenty-three years later!

Workington got through their tricky away FA Cup tie at Scarborough with a 3-2 win. Jeff Barmby and George Siddle scored for the hosts, but a Tommy Spratt double and a goal from Jimmy Goodfellow sealed the tie for Reds.

Billy Watson kept Borough Park in pristine condition for 38 years, and the pitch was frequently praised by visiting teams. Watson was groundsman at Workington from 12 January 1952 – the day Reds played Liverpool at Anfield in the FA Cup – until 1989, and he was awarded a testimonial in 1980.

Les Massie (*left*) and Alan Tyrer. Massie joined Workington in 1969, having played for Huddersfield, and was subsequently a Fourth Division top scorer with Halifax in 1967/68. His experience was an asset to Workington during some difficult seasons, and he scored 15 goals in 62 Football League appearances between 1969 and 1971.

George Aitken returned to Borough Park to manage Workington in the 1971/72 season. Operating on a shoestring budget, the former Reds star performed a miracle in steering the club to sixth place in the Fourth Division. This programme is for the game against Stockport on 19 February 1972 that finished 1-1 – part of a 6-match unbeaten run.

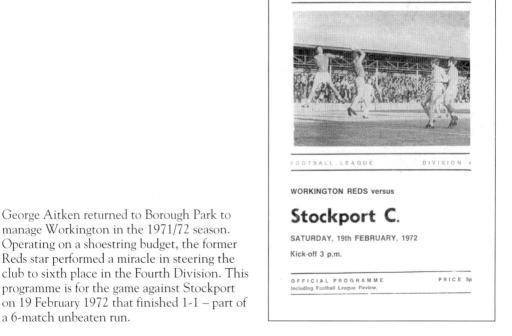

WORKINGTON   ASSOCIATION   FOOTBALL   CLUB

BOROUGH PARK   ·   WORKINGTON

FOOTBALL LEAGUE   DIVISION 4

WORKINGTON REDS versus

Stockport C.

SATURDAY, 19th FEBRUARY, 1972

Kick-off 3 p.m.

OFFICIAL PROGRAMME   PRICE 5p
Including Football League Peview.

WORKINGTON

VERSUS

DARLINGTON

FOOTBALL LEAGUE	DIVISION FOUR

OFFICIAL PROGRAMME 5p   with Football League Review

Saturday, 23rd Sept., 1972   **Kick Off 3 p.m.**

BOROUGH PARK   WORKINGTON

The 1972/73 campaign proved difficult, but excellent home form – Reds lost just one League game at Borough Park – ensured that Workington finished a respectable thirteenth in the Fourth Division.

Nine
Decline and Fall
1973-1977

Dave Murray scores in the 4-1 win over Peterborough United at Borough Park on 24 February 1974. Although Workington's home form was not too bad, just one away win ensured that Reds finished second bottom of the Fourth Division in 1973/74 and they had to apply for re-election.

Paul Murray is outnumbered by Reading defenders during the 0-0 draw at Borough Park on 27 October 1973. Workington began the season well and suffered just 4 League defeats up to the start of November.

Tony Geidmintis and groundsman Billy Watson at Borough Park. Geidmintis made his debut for Workington in 1964 at the age of fifteen and stayed at the club until 1976, making 323 Football League appearances.

One of the biggest problems that Workington faced was a serious decline in attendances. Seven League matches in 1973/74 drew crowds of under 1,000, with just 693 turning out for the visit of Exeter City on 15 December 1973. The terraces tell their own story during this game against Doncaster on 10 February 1974.

Dave Helliwell (7) on the attack for Reds during the 4-1 defeat of Peterborough on 24 February 1974. Helliwell had played for Blackburn Rovers and Lincoln City before coming to Workington, where he settled down for six years and played the best football of his career. The midfielder made 184 Football League appearances for Workington.

Keith Skillen (*left*) flies high during the 0-0 draw against Mansfield Town on 15 April 1974. Despite finishing twenty-third in the Fourth Division, Reds' reasonable performances and the fact that it was their first re-election bid since 1968 ensured they received 21 votes – 5 more than Kettering Town – but the fairly narrow margin was a warning of things to come.

Groundsman Billy Watson's affection for cats meant that a posse of felines occupied Borough Park throughout his tenure. This individual, known as 'Blackie', had a tendency to take a leisurely stroll across the halfway line during matches and hold up play!

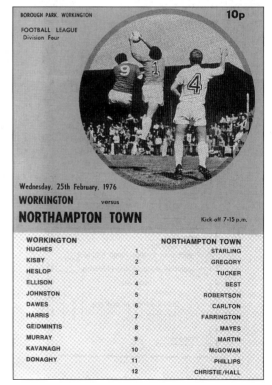

BOROUGH PARK, WORKINGTON

FOOTBALL LEAGUE
Division Four

10p

Wednesday, 25th February, 1976

WORKINGTON versus

NORTHAMPTON TOWN

Kick-off 7-15 p.m.

WORKINGTON		NORTHAMPTON TOWN
HUGHES	1	STARLING
KISBY	2	GREGORY
HESLOP	3	TUCKER
ELLISON	4	BEST
JOHNSTON	5	ROBERTSON
DAWES	6	CARLTON
HARRIS	7	FARRINGTON
GEIDMINTIS	8	MAYES
MURRAY	9	MARTIN
KAVANAGH	10	McGOWAN
DONAGHY	11	PHILLIPS
	12	CHRISTIE/HALL

The 1975/76 season turned out to be one of severe struggle, with just 7 wins and 21 points obtained. However, Workington were given another chance at the Football League AGM, polling 21 votes to Yeovil Town's 18. Surprise away wins at Hartlepool and Newport County in the last two games of the season may just have tipped the balance in Workington's favour.

A bright spot in the 1975/76 season was the form of Malcolm Dawes (*second from the right*) which earned him the Supporters' Association's inaugural Player of the Year award. Pictured with Dawes are Alan Ashman (manager), Tony Geidmintis, Martin Harris and Steve Durham (Supporters' Association chairman).

John Honour, Barry Donaghy and Eamon Kavanagh training at Borough Park. At the start of the 1976/77 season, it really was do or die for Workington if they were to retain their Football League status, which was now hanging by a slender thread.

Workington AFC, 1976/77. From left to right, back row: Jackie Cunningham (physiotherapist), Ray Ellison, Ian Johnston, Graham Monkhouse, Mike Rogan, Phil Ashworth, Bobby Brown, Eamon Kavanagh, Paddy Lowrey, Alan Ashman (manager). Front row: Mike Higgins, John Honour, Barry Donaghy, Malcolm Dawes, Mick Leng, Chris Kisby, Martin Harris.

To his great credit, Mike Rogan stayed with Workington for the 1976/77 season. The goalkeeper's acrobatics were often all that saved his side from a mauling, as results quickly made it apparent that the club faced a hopeless task in trying to climb off the bottom of the table.

Locally-born Graham Monkhouse (*left*) deputised in goal for Mike Rogan on 5 occasions for Workington during 1976/77. He later became a successful all-rounder at cricket for Surrey from 1981 to 1985, and has recently been player-coach at Wigton Cricket Club. Phil Ashworth (*right*) gave his all for Reds in a dismal 1976/77 season. He played 38 games, both as a defender and forward, and scored Workington's last Football League goal – an 89th-minute penalty against Stockport County on 4 May 1977.

Workington went into their last two games – both against Newport County – destined to finish bottom of the Fourth Division, while Newport were staging a revival to lift them out of the re-election zone. Newport won the first match, played at Borough Park, 1-0 on 14 May 1977.

Three days later, Newport reproduced the same scoreline at Somerton Park. It was 'The Great Escape' for Newport, but not for Reds.

Skipper Chris Kisby leads Phil Ashworth and John Honour out for Workington's last Football League match at Newport on 17 May 1977.

Martin Scholes and Ian Johnston battle to the last during the 1-0 defeat at Newport County on 17 May 1977. Exactly one month later, at the Football League AGM, Wimbledon received 37 votes to Workington's 27. Workington AFC were no longer a Football League club.

Ten
Non-League Life
1977-1986

Workington players and fans celebrate winning the Northern Premier League President's Cup in 1984. Captain John Reach holds the trophy, with manager Joe Wojciechowicz in the bottom right of the picture.

Life goes on. New player-manager Gordon Livsey was one of several fresh faces for Workington's first season in the Northern Premier League. From left to right, back row: Mickey Wardrop, George Thompson, Neil McDonald, Gordon Livsey, Mick Leng, Martin Scholes, Keith Skillen. Front row: Ian Johnston, Tony Moore, Jimmy Irving, Bobby Brown, Billy Smith, Terry Davies, Ian Hodgson.

Workington found anything but respite from struggle in the Northern Premier League. Reds went through two managers, Gordon Livsey and David Wilson, and could only finish nineteenth in the table.

Goalkeeper Gerard Fisher receives the 1978 Player of the Year award from Supporters' Assocation chairman Steve Durham.

Crowds return to Borough Park. After a grim 1979/80 season, when Workington finished second bottom of the Northern Premier League, a welcome boost came in 1980/81, as Reds drew local rivals Carlisle United in the first round of the FA Cup. Carlisle fans make their way from the railway station to Borough Park.

The attendance becomes 7,362 … less one as a fan is ejected from Borough Park during the FA Cup tie against Carlisle. The match finished 0-0 as Reds forced a replay at Brunton Park.

Mick Hill, Wayne Roberts (5) and John Reach on the defence for Workington in the 0-0 draw against Carlisle United on 22 November 1980.

Action from the FA Cup first round replay between Carlisle United and Workington. Carlisle ran out 4-1 winners, but the matches provided Reds with a welcome boost in terms of publicity and finance.

Bill Shankly returned to Workington in 1981 to open the new Shankly Lounge beneath the grandstand. Workington chairman Arthur McCullogh holds the inaugural pint.

Programme editor Steve Durham (*centre*) with Tom Meldrum, Peter Winkworth, Arthur McCullough and Colin Doorbar, after Reds' programme was voted the best in the Northern Premier League for 1980/81. The season saw improvement all round, with Workington pushing up to a final position of tenth.

Groundsman Billy Watson completed thirty years of service at Borough Park in 1982. Here he receives a special award to commemorate the milestone from Northern Premier League secretary Duncan Bayley.

Borough Park captured in the gloom of a winter's evening. The perimeter of Lonsdale Park –
Reds' former home, and, at this point, still used for greyhound racing – can be seen on the right.

Workington eventually found some stability under manager Joe Wojciechowicz and, in 1982/83, they finished seventh in the Northern Premier League, qualifying for the President's Cup. Reds beat Chorley and Burton Albion to reach the two-legged final against Marine. After drawing 1-1 at Marine, Workington drew a tense match at Borough Park 0-0 to win the trophy on away goals. Skipper John Reach lifts the President's Cup – Workington's first significant trophy since winning the North-Eastern League Challenge Cup in 1937.

Workington had every reason to celebrate after 1,125 fans saw them achieve tangible success at last, following years of struggle. From left to right: John Smith, Vaughn Williams, John Reach, Martin Harris, Wayne Harrison.

John Reach and groundsman Billy Watson keep a tight hold on the President's Cup at Borough Park in 1984.

Striker John Smith in action against Rhyl in 1984/85, a season in which Workington finished eighth in the Northern Premier League.

John Smith was instrumental in reviving Workington's fortunes in the early to mid-1980s and, on 31 March 1985, he became the club's first post-war player to score 100 goals for Reds. Smith is presented with a bronze boot by Joan Crellin of the Supporters' Association to mark the achievement.

Manager Wayne Harrison introduces Nat Lofthouse to Kevin Rowntree before Workington's pre-season friendly against Bolton Wanderers on 29 July 1985. Harrison cut his managerial teeth at Borough Park before going on to Lancaster City, Bamber Bridge and Accrington Stanley, as well as another spell at Workington in 1995. He is now director of coaching at Eden Prairie Soccer Club in the United States and has his own website, http://waynesworld-of-soccer.com, having written books on advanced football coaching techniques.

John Smith in action in a high-scoring FA Trophy match against Brandon United on
2 November 1985. Reds ran out 5-4 winners.

George Best (*right*) with player-manager Wayne Harrison at Borough Park on 9 April 1986. Best guested for Reds in a fund-raising match against a Lancashire Football League XI.

George Best in action for Workington. The game against the Lancashire Football League XI finished 1-1 in front of a crowd of 3,500.

Billy Gilmour receives the 1986 Player of the Year award from the Northern Premier League's Ken Marsden. Another reasonable season in 1985/86 saw Workington again finish eighth.

Eleven

Nadir

1986-1998

With attendances down to below 200 by the mid-1990s, Workington faced an almost daily struggle for survival – what a sorry contrast to the heady days of the late 1950s and early 1960s. Note the truncated floodlight pylon. (*Picture courtesy of www.homesoffootball.co.uk*)

Workington lost 2-0 to Manchester United in a pre-season friendly at Borough Park on 9 August 1986. Mark Dobie is foiled by United goalkeeper Fraser Digby.

Workington made a brief return to Lonsdale Park for five games in 1986/87 because safety work needed to be carried out at Borough Park. Mark Dobie wins the ball in a 1-1 draw with Burton Albion on 13 December 1986, with Alan Kamara back-tracking for Burton.

Wayne Harrison on the ball against Billingham Synthonia on 13 September 1986. The 1986/87 season proved grim, with Reds finishing second bottom of the Northern Premier League with just 5 wins from 42 matches. However, they retained their place in the newly-formed Northern Premier League Premier Division for the following season.

With Borough Park's elegant grandstand deemed unsafe for spectators in 1988, the club simply removed the roof and seating in order to save the club's facilities in the buildings below.

The removal of the grandstand in 1988 marked a new low in Workington's fortunes, both off and on the pitch. In 1987/88, the team finished bottom of the Northern Premier League Premier Division and were relegated to the Northern Premier League First Division, renamed the HFS Loans League from 1988.

Garry Messenger (*left*) wins a tackle during a 3-0 home defeat by Newtown during the 1988/89 season. Workington showed no sign of being able to launch a promotion push with a final placing of sixteenth in the HFS Loans League First Division in 1988/89, and they even finished bottom of the First Division in 1990/91.

REDS REVIEW
The Monthly Magazine for Supporters of Workington AFC

No. 4. JUNE 1992.   £1.00

REDS' GREATEST DAY: 25th April 1964 – photographs are taken before the 0-0 draw with Exeter City which secured promotion to the 3rd Division.

FROM THE GLORIES OF THE PAST WE MUST DRAW INSPIRATION FOR THE STRUGGLES OF THE PRESENT

By 1992, the only bright spot was the launch of a monthly supporters' magazine, *Reds Review*. However, this cover, depicting the promotion side of 1964, could not have contrasted more starkly with the club's fortunes in the summer of 1992. Having finished bottom of the HFS Loans League First Division, Workington faced relegation yet again and were in danger of extinction. Irlam Town's resignation from the division earned Workington a reprieve, and a crisis over being able to stay at Borough Park was also averted.

Sean Sunderland scores in a 1-1 draw against Netherfield at Borough Park on 31 August 1992. Reds at least managed to lift themselves to mid-table anonymity with a league placing of thirteenth in 1992/93.

Billy Gilmour (*right*) is involved in a midfield tussle with Tony Monaghan during Reds' first win on Scottish soil – a 2-1 league success over Gretna in August 1993.

Martin Henderson was the main source of much-needed goals in the mid-1990s. He was the club's top-scorer for three successive seasons, with 22 goals in 1993/94, 22 in 1994/95 and 21 in 1995/96.

Graham Caton (*right*) in action against Harrogate Town during the 1993/94 season, which again saw Workington in the comfort zone with an eleventh-place finish.

Paddy Atkinson (*right*) chases a ball in the 2-1 win over Eastwood Town on 5 March 1994. Having started his career with Sheffield United, Atkinson later moved back into the Football League with York City and Scarborough, before joining Queen of the South.

Wayne Harrison (*right*), back at Borough Park, is poised to challenge against Warrington Town's Joey Dunn in the last game of the 1994/95 season on 2 May 1995. Workington had to win or they faced relegation from what was by now the Unibond League Division One. Trailing by 2-0, Reds stormed back to win 3-2.

The FA Cup failed to provide much relief during the relentless struggle that was the story of the first eight years of the 1990s at Borough Park. Martin Henderson prepares to shoot in a 4-2 defeat by Spennymoor United during 1995/96.

Darren Wilson (*right*) keeps his eye on the ball in Workington's record 7-1 FA Trophy win at Rothwell Town in the third qualifying round on 30 November 1996. However, Reds were on the receiving end in the first round proper when they crashed 5-2 at home to Bamber Bridge.

John Burridge's final appearance at Borough Park was twenty-six years after he left the club. He played for Blyth Spartans in a pre-season friendly on 16 August 1997, and is seen here with his sister Marion Hyde.

Reds' Jeff Henderson (*left*) and Paul Farley in a 1-1 draw at Lincoln United on 28 February 1998. The 1997/98 season finally brought about what had threatened to happen for several years – Workington finished second bottom of the Unibond League First Division and were relegated to the North-West Trains League – four divisions below the Football League.

Twelve

Champions at Last
1998-1999

Champagne celebrations after Workington beat Mossley 2-1 to lift the North-West Trains League championship and secure promotion back to the Unibond League at the first attempt.

Borough Park's home dressing room at the start of the 1998/99 season. The room that had seen sides prepare for classic games against Manchester United, Blackburn Rovers and Chelsea would now prelude North-West Trains League football with the likes of Ramsbottom United and Atherton Collieries providing rather less illustrious opposition.

Paul Stewart's signing was a huge boost to the squad. The former England international prepares to make his debut at Prescot Cables on 12 September 1998.

An extraordinary run of 13 consecutive victories lifted Reds up to second in the table and meant that victory over league leaders Mossley on the last day of the season would secure the championship. Crowds queue outside Borough Park to buy advance tickets for what was to be a 2,281 sell-out.

Stuart Williamson heads home against Mossley to calm Reds' nerves in the final match of the season on 3 May 1999. Grant Holt then added a second, and Workington held on to win the North West Trains League and clinch a return to the Unibond League.

Skipper Martin Kirkby holds the North-West Trains League championship trophy aloft. It was the first major championship in the club's history, and Reds' performances re-ignited interest in Workington AFC throughout the town and beyond.

122

Thirteen
Towards a
Brighter Future
1999-2003

Barry Irving scoring at Gretna in a 3-1 victory on 8 January 2000. Workington finished in fifteenth position, but well clear of the relegation places, in their first season back in the Unibond League.

Workington won the Cumberland Cup for the twenty-second time in 2000, with a 2-0 win over Carlisle United at Borough Park. Manager Peter Hampton (*front*) leads the celebrations, as Graeme Carr holds the trophy.

Alan Gray, Billy Barr and Mark Jones in action during the 1-0 defeat by Ossett Town at Borough Park on 20 March 2001. Reds finished the 2000/01 season in fourteenth place in the Unibond League First Division.

Alec Graham presents defender Alan Gray with the National Supporters' Club Player of the Year award for 2001. Gray joined Workington from Carlisle at the start of the 1998/99 season, and was a regular at full-back before moving to Queen of the South in 2001.

After a poor start to the 2001/02 season, Peter Hampton was sacked and former Newcastle United and Northern Ireland international Tommy Cassidy was appointed manager. Cassidy, seen receiving a Fair Play Team of the Month award from League vice-president Gerry Jones, steadily steered Reds away from the relegation zone to a final position of sixteenth.

Will Varty collects a Man of the Match award from Workington vice chairman Humphrey Dobie in September 2002. Varty, a former Carlisle United regular, was one of Tommy Cassidy's major signings as he looked to push Reds towards the right end of the Unibond League First Division table in 2002/03.

Andy Mullen (*centre*), who played in Reds' first Football League match, still watches Workington whenever they play in the east of England. He is seen with travelling companions Roger Irving and Tom Allen.

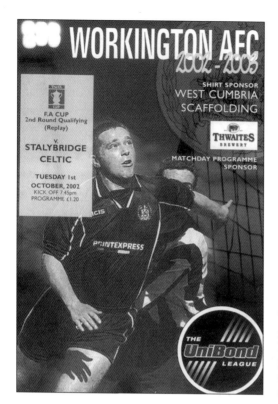

Workington's 42-page match programme for 2002/03 would put many Football League publications to shame. It is professionally presented and right up to date, featuring a wealth of interesting articles and photographs.

The Town End at Borough Park has changed precious little since Workington's Football League home debut on 22 August 1951. The ground suffered from decay for many years, but it is now kept in pristine condition despite a tight budget. For those who have not already made the trip, a visit to this fascinating football outpost is highly recommended.

Further Reading and Viewing

Several books have covered various aspects of Workington's history, though many are currently out of print. A couple of exceptions are Tom Allen's *The Team Beyond The Hills*, which provides thirty biographies of notable players from 1951 to 1977, with numerous illustrations. This 96-page publication can be obtained from the author at 126 Oxford Street, Cleethorpes, NE Lincolnshire, DN35 0BP.

Workington programme editor and match secretary Steve Durham produced an illustrated book *Workington AFC – 1998/99*, charting the North-West Trains League championship season. This 66-page work is available direct from the author at 10 Grant Drive, Bleach Green, Whitehaven, Cumbria. CA28 6JS. Steve Durham also produced a centenary brochure *Workington AFC 1884-1984*, packed with interesting facts and figures. This is long since out of print and very difficult to track down.

During the early 1990s, Martin Wingfield self-published a three-volume brochure-style book *So Sad, So Very Sad* covering the Football League history of Workington. Part one covers 1951-1958 with an extra pictorial supplement, part two is about the period 1958-1964, while part three focuses solely on the 1964/65 season. The series was never completed, so there are no volumes beyond that point. All are out of print, but copies may be in stock at Wallace & Scott Books, 9 Oxford Street, Workington, Cumbria, CA14 2AL.

Archive videos of Football League matches featuring Workington are almost impossible to find with one exception. The Yore Publications video *Rejected FC* features colour footage of Workington's last home Football League game in May 1977 against Newport County. Contact Yore Publications, 12 The Furrows, Harefield, Middlesex, UB9 6AT.